THE TIGER/CRANE FORM
of Hung Gar Kung-Fu

by Bucksam Kong

Editor: Gregory Lee
Graphic Design: Karen Mass?

Art Production: Mary Schepis

© 1983 Ohara Publications, Inc.
All rights reserved
Printed in the United States of America
Library of Congress Catalog Card Number: 83-60126
ISBN: 0-89750-087-3

Tenth printing 1995

WARNING

OHARA PUBLICATIONS, INCORPORATED

SANTA CLARITA, CALIFORNIA

Standing (left to right): Corey
Chuck, Steve Munizich
and Andrew Kong.
Seated: Bucksam Kong

This book is dedicated to my son Andrew. It often seems that because of my own involvement and commitments to kung-fu that I don't always have enough time to teach my son. However, I want him to know that kung-fu is something that cannot be handed down from father to son. Success in kung-fu can only be achieved through dedication and self-sacrifice. After 15 years, my son finally asked me to teach him, and I know that when he wants to learn, he will. I want to teach all who are sincere in their desire to learn.

About the Author

Bucksam Kong is one of the foremost experts in the West on the Hung Gar style of kung fu, the system of the "five-formed fist." He is chief instructor of the Sil Lum Pai Gung Fu Association, and foreign advisor to both the Hong Kong Chinese Martial Arts Association and the Hong Kong Choy Li Fut Association.

A *Black Belt* Hall of Fame member (1974), Kong has studied the intricate fighting systems of China all his life, beginning with his instructor in Hong Kong, Lum Jo. Kong has been a preserver of one of the most popular of all kung fu styles, and the one generally accepted as closest to the original chuan fa of the ancient Shaolin temple.

Kong taught kung fu in Hawaii for 20 years before moving to Los Angeles, California, in 1977 with his wife Nancy and their three children. His first book, *Hung Gar Kung Fu: Chinese Art of Self-Defense,* was published by Ohara Publications in 1973.

Preface

I deliberated for many years on the idea of communicating the tiger crane set of kung-fu through the medium of a book. What has made this a difficult decision is the tradition of the practitioners of this kung-fu style to frown on public exposure to this knowledge. Because of my desire to share this knowledge with dedicated kung-fu practitioners, I have finally decided to go ahead with this project. No part of this set, *fu hok sheong yin kuen*, has been omitted or withheld.

The tiger crane set is the most valuable set in the hung gar style. It covers every angle and contains both long- and short-range techniques, as well as a combination of hard and soft techniques. The versatility of its techniques are such that the usage of this set is virtually unlimited (in its self-defense qualities).

The study of hung gar cannot be complete without learning this entire set. It provides a path by which the student can gain an understanding of sophisticated hand movements. It opens the door to enlightenment and prepares the student for successful training in kung-fu.

I would like to thank my wife, Shuk Han Kong, for her love and moral support; Roger Yano, for his hard work in helping me assemble this book; my very good students who spent long hours in the studio posing for these photographs; and the staff of Ohara Publications for all their help.

—Bucksam Kong
December, 1982
Los Angeles, California

Historical Origins

The tiger/crane set is an element of the hung gar kung-fu style. This style traces its origins back to Hung Hee Gung during the era of the Ching Dynasty.

During this time the Ching armies destroyed the Shaolin temple. A single monk, Chee Sin, survived Shaolin's destruction. Hung Hee Gung became one of his students. Hung was a very strong man, and the tiger fighting techniques were particularly suited to him. He soon became famed for his fighting prowess.

During his travels he met a woman, Fong Wing Chun, who had developed her own fighting techniques based on the movements of a crane. According to legend, one day a crane began eating Fong's rice as it was being dried. She tried to drive the crane off with a stick, but the crane was too agile and elusive. No matter how hard she tried, Fong found that she was unable to strike the crane. She then began to study the crane's motions in order to understand how it was able to evade her attacks. She later developed fighting techniques based on these motions.

Before Hung and Fong met, her father was killed by a very strong fighter (whose name has been lost in time). She knew that, by herself, she could not hope to defeat her father's killer. When she met Hung—he was already a famous fighter—she convinced him that even though he had great strength and powerful fighting techniques, to be a more complete martial artist he should learn some evasive techniques. She offered to teach him her crane techniques in return for his help in seeking revenge on her father's killer.

Hung agreed and spent the next three years perfecting a union of the tiger and crane techniques, which he later used to defeat the killer of Fong's father.

This is the history of how tiger/crane was created.

How To Use This Book

This volume presents the tiger/crane set *(fu hok sheong yin kuen)* in its entirety, using 268 separate photographs. The form is also broken down in a unique way that allows the student to study the practical self-defense applications of every move in this form.

The first time you study this book, examine the entire form first from front to back (the steps are numbered consecutively throughout this book), skipping the application sections at first. Then go back and begin again with the first section of the form, the Opening Salute. Now turn the page and notice the photographs and caption for the application of these moves. For every section and step of this form, there is a corresponding page immediately after that demonstrates the actual combat possibilities of each move, including situations against more than one opponent.

It is possible to study this book again and again, reviewing sequences of the tiger/crane set that you may have forgotten, or looking up the self-defense applications of certain steps.

No art form can be completely mastered through book instruction. Once you have studied the tiger/crane set, personal instruction can help bring out its more intangible benefits. Perserverance and hard work are the key.

CONTENTS

Striking Hands

The hand weapons used in the tiger/crane set of hung gar kung-fu are many. They are depicted here close-up so that your hands can be formed in the required configurations as they are called for throughout the text. Note carefully the positions of the fingers, thumb and wrist with each hand or fist. The heel of the palm, the tips of the fingers, the front and back knuckles and the elbow are all used effectively for strikes in hung gar.

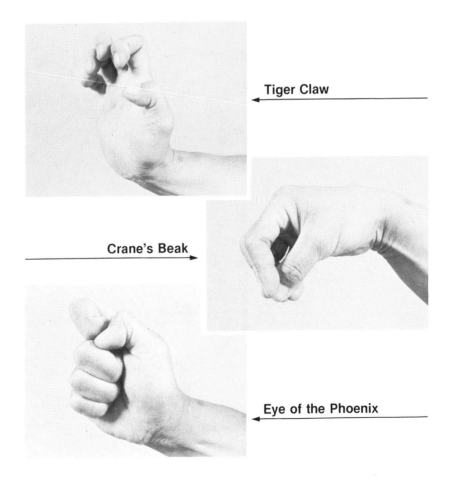

Tiger Claw

Crane's Beak

Eye of the Phoenix

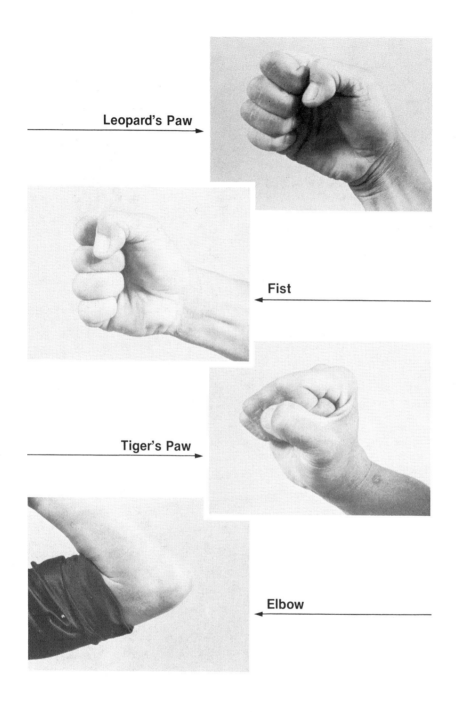

Leopard's Paw

Fist

Tiger's Paw

Elbow

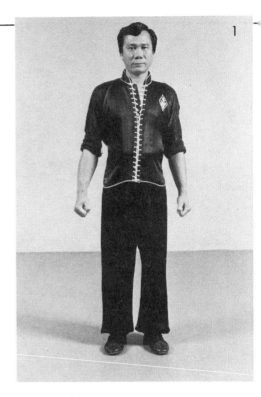

TiqER/CRANE
FORM
(Opening Salute)

(1) Stand in a relaxed posture, arms straight at your sides and your feet close together. (2) Assume the ready position by drawing your fists up to your waist, palms up. (3) Step forward with your right foot, crossing the right leg in front of your left leg into a scissors stance. At the same time, execute a palm block (left to right) with your left hand. (4) Move your left leg forward into a cat stance, at the same time drawing your left hand back from right to left (palm out) while executing a right punch. (5) Bring both fists inward toward your chest. (6) Retract your left leg back to the ready postion while moving both your left and right fists in a downward arc to your waist. (Steps 1-6 complete the opening salute.)

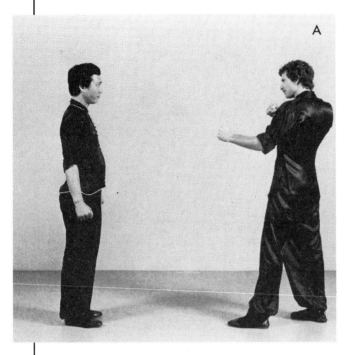

APPLICATION

(A&B) Your opponent steps forward and executes a straight punch with his right hand. (C) Step forward with your right foot into a scissors stance and simultaneously execute a palm block with your left hand, deflecting the punch

to your right. (D) Use your left hand to push your opponent's fist outward while at the same time moving your left leg forward into a cat stance and executing a straight right punch to your opponent's solar plexus.

FORM

(Throughout this sequence, your feet and your left fist will remain stationary.) (7) Move your right hand up to eye level and rotate the palm down in a counterclockwise direction, executing a downward palm block. (8) Move your right hand up in a clockwise motion, elbow bent, palm facing in. This is a forearm block. (9) Move your right hand horizontally (from right to left) across your chest. Your palm should now point away from your body. (10) Move your right hand downward in a diagonal sweeping motion across your abdomen and back to your hip (palm down). (11) Move your right hand up in a diagonal sweeping motion (right to left) to chin level, palm out. (12) Without moving your elbow, straighten your right arm horizontally until your palm faces out away from you. This is a palm heel strike.

APPLICATION

(A) As your opponent moves in with a right punch, execute a downward palm block with your right hand. (B) As your opponent counters with a left punch, move your right hand in a clockwise motion to execute an inside fore-

arm block. (C&D) As your opponent throws another right punch, use your right hand to execute a horizontal palm block. (E) Execute a palm heel strike with your right hand to your opponent's face.

13

14

17

18

FORM

(13) Retract your right hand straight back toward your right shoulder and breath in through your nose simultaneously. (14&15) Push your right palm forward again, exhaling through your mouth. Repeat steps 13-15 once more. Now retract your right palm toward your right ear, at the same time, raising your right elbow so that your right forearm is now parallel to the floor (not shown). Now drop your elbow in a downward arc until it is a hand's span from your chest and thrust (16) your right hand straight out (palm down). Bending only at the wrist, move your hand left to

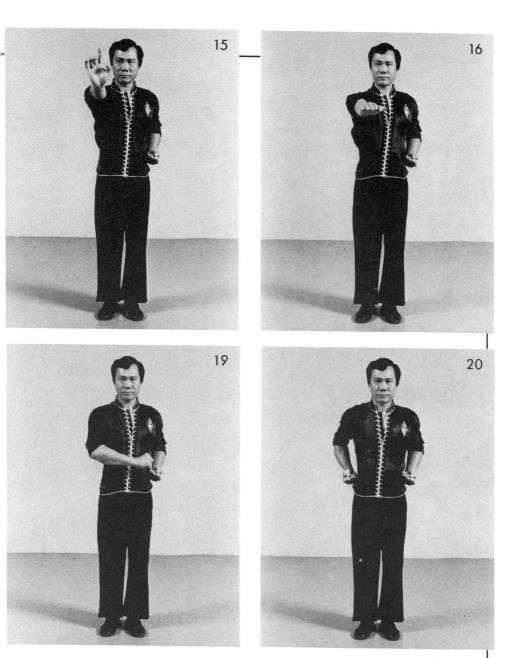

right four times. On the fourth motion, rotate (17) your wrist clockwise until your fingers point upward and your palm is facing you. Bending only at the wrist, rotate (18) your hand counterclockwise until your palm faces down, then form a tiger claw with your right hand. Your wrist should pull down with a snapping action and your palm will be pointed away from you. (19) Form a fist and execute a downward block with your right forearm. (20) Retract your right fist back to your waist in the ready position. Now repeat steps 7-20 with your left hand.

A

B

APPLICATION

(A) As your opponent steps in with a left punch, (B) raise your right hand toward your right ear, blocking to the outside with the outer edge of your wrist and forearm. (C) As he

counters with a right punch, drop your right hand and forearm straight down delivering a palm heel block. (D) Deliver a finger strike to your opponent's eyes.

FORM

(21) In rapid succession, execute a right punch at chest level followed by (22) a left punch at chest level while retracting your right fist. (23) Retract your left fist to the ready position.

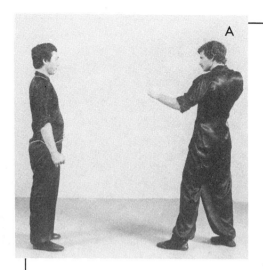

APPLICATION

(A) As your opponent threatens with a right punch to your chest, (B) use a left forearm block to deflect his fist down and away (step 19 when repeated using the left hand). (C&D) Counter immediately with a right straight punch to your opponent's face and a left straight punch to his solar plexus.

24

25

FORM

Swing your right leg outward in a low circular (clockwise) movement, then swing your left leg (counterclockwise) in the same fashion, planting your feet into the horse stance. (You should perform these two steps so that you do not have to shift your feet again to find the proper position.) After you have assumed the horse stance, (24) thrust both fists directly upward from the waist in an arc. Your fists should be at eye level, shoulder-width apart. (25) Simultaneously, thrust both elbows backward to your sides. Your elbow, bicep and shoulder should now form a straight line.

APPLICATION

(A) Your opponent approaches from behind and attempts to encircle your arms in a bear hug. (B) Drop your weight into a horse stance while simultaneously raising both fists in an upward arc, loosening or breaking your opponent's hold. (C) Reach across your chest with your left hand and grab your opponent's right wrist. (D) Raise your opponent's arm and pivot to your right underneath, delivering an elbow strike to his ribs.

25

FORM

(26) Open both fists and thrust downward at a 45-degree angle away from your body. (27) Move your left forearm up in a counterclockwise motion. (28) Move your right forearm up in a clockwise motion. (*Note:* In these last two steps, notice the configuration of the hand; all but the first finger are curved in toward the palm.) (29) Draw both palms back toward your shoulders, simultaneously inhaling through your nose. (30) Push both palms forward to their position in step 28, at the same time forcing your breath down below your navel. As you reach full extension, exhale through your mouth. Now repeat steps 29 and 30 two more times.

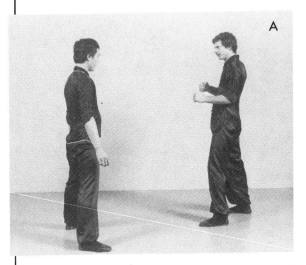

APPLICATION

(A&B) As your opponent attempts a right front kick to your groin, drop down into a horse stance and execute a downward forearm block with your left arm. Your forearm should contact the inside of your opponent's leg, deflecting it out away from you. (C) As your opponent steps in with a right punch, circle

your left hand up in a counterclockwise motion to block his fist to the outside. (D) As he counters with a left punch, circle your right hand up in a clockwise motion to block his fist to the outside. (E) Execute a thrust with both palms to your opponent's chest to throw him off balance.

FORM

(31) Draw both forearms back in an upward arc, your palms past your ears. (32) Drop both forearms in a downward arc until they are parallel with the ground. (33) Thrust both arms straight out, palms down.

APPLICATION

(A) Your opponent threatens with a straight right punch. (B) Drop into a horse stance, simultaneously bringing your left forearm down on your opponent's punch, deflecting it downward. (C) Thrust both hands forward in a strike to your opponent's eyes.

FORM

(34) Snap both wrists downward such that both hands now form the tiger's claw. (35) Swing both arms horizontally to your left. (36) Pivot your upper body back, then retract both arms toward your shoulders. (37) Thrust both palms straight out, arms parallel to the ground. (38-40) Repeat steps 35-37 but on the opposite side.

A

APPLICATION

(A) As your opponent throws a straight right punch, (B) swing both arms in a horizontal arc, from left to right, deflecting his punch. (C) Step with your right foot toward your opponent, using your right

B

hand to maintain control of his punching arm, and place your left hand on his shoulder. (D) Take a half step forward and thrust with both hands, throwing your opponent off balance.

FORM

(41) Rotate both forearms away from your body and thrust with both hands upward at a 45-degree angle away from your body. (42) Swing both arms downward in a semicircle (your left hand moves counterclockwise, your right hand clockwise). Your palms should be turned up, left over right. (43) Repeat step 41 (note the hand configuration). (44) Drop both forearms straight down so that they are parallel to the ground. (45) Thrust both arms straight out, palms down. (46) Drop your elbows, at the same time, rotate your forearms until your palms are facing each other. (47) Rotate your palms toward your body until the fingers are pointed at your chest.

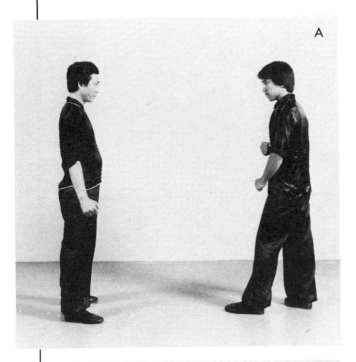

A

B

APPLICATION

(A&B) Your opponent attempts a choke hold. (C) Step forward and simultaneously raise both hands inside your opponent's forearms thrusting out-

ward, breaking his hold. (D) Swing both arms down and in, palms up, striking your opponent's neck with both hands.

FORM

(48) Rotate your right forearm counterclockwise until it is parallel with the ground. Rotate your left forearm until it is parallel with the ground (your right arm should be closest to your body). Pivot to your left into a forward stance, simultaneously pushing your left hand outward and striking with a right hand tiger claw. (49) Rotate your right hand counterclockwise until it is parallel with the ground and (50) pivot to your right into a forward stance and execute another tiger claw strike using the left hand (the right hand pushes outward, just the reverse of step 48).

APPLICATION

(A&B) As your opponent throws a straight right punch, use your right forearm to deflect the punch to your left. (C) As you rotate the trunk of your body to the right, simultaneously use your right palm to grab and pull your opponent's arm to your right. (D) Execute a tiger claw strike to your opponent's face with your left hand. The block, parry and strike should be one, smooth motion.

FORM

(51) Drop your right hand down to your right hip while retracting your left hand across your chest. (52) Pivot back into a horse stance, moving your right palm from right to left toward your left hip and slightly outward from your body. Your right palm stays in the same relative position as step 51.

APPLICATION

(A) Your opponent approaches from your left side throwing a left punch to your head. (B) Pivot to your left while raising your left forearm to block and parry his punch up and to your left. (C) Drop into a horse stance and use the edge of your right palm to strike your opponent's midsection.

FORM

(53) Rotate your left forearm (not shown) counterclockwise, performing an outside circular block, then rotate your right forearm clockwise to perform an outside circular block. Perform three blocks one after the other for each arm. (54&55) Jump straight up with both feet, raising your fists high (palms in) and bringing them down simultaneously in an arc, landing in a standing position. Your fists are palms up at the waist.

APPLICATION

(A) As your opponent throws a right punch, (B&C) jump up raising both fists simultaneously over your head, delivering strikes to your opponent's upper arm and head as you come down.

FORM

(56) Step forward with your left leg as you pivot 45 degrees to your right into a scissors stance. (57&58) Bring your right leg up and across your body, then thrust your leg out at knee level.

APPLICATION

(A&B) As your opponent throws a right front kick to your groin, bring your right leg up quickly across your body, using your shin to deflect his kick. (C) Thrust your right foot immediately at his exposed left knee.

FORM

(59) From step 58, cock your right leg again, then step out into a forward stance, still facing 45 degrees to your right. At the same time, thrust your left palm down in an arc. (60) Rotate your left forearm counterclockwise until your palm is directly in front of your body. (61) Retract your left palm toward your left shoulder. (62) Thrust your left palm straight out. Repeat steps 61 and 62 two more times. (63) Draw your left palm in an upward arc until your palm is near your left ear. (64) Thurst your left forearm in a downward arc until it is parallel with the ground. (65) Thrust your left hand straight out, fully extending your left arm until your fingers are at eye level. (66) Snap your wrist downward, forming the tiger claw. Bend your elbow at the same time. (67) With your feet remaining in place, shift back into a horse stance, simultaneously raising the right palm clockwise across your chest blocking outward, 45 degrees to your right. At the same time, retract your left hand into a ready position at the waist. (68) Shift back into a right forward stance, simultaneously thrusting straight out with a left tiger claw. Your right fist is drawn back into the ready position. Note that the left elbow is not fully extended.

APPLICATION

(A) Counter an opponent's right punch to your mid-section by sliding your left foot back into a right forward stance and using your left palm to deflect his fist downward. (B) Thrust your left hand up and out in a finger strike to your opponent's throat. (C&D) If he evades the finger strike

and attempts to counter with a left punch to the face, shift back into a horse stance and deflect his punch outward with a right forearm block (ideally, C&D should be performed simultaneously). (E) Follow up with a tiger claw strike to your opponent's abdomen.

FORM

(69) Shift into a horse stance, simultaneously moving the right palm across in a downward block and drawing the left fist back to your waist. (70) Lift your right forearm up and outward, then (71) swing your right forearm in a downward arc to your left, palm up at chest level.

APPLICATION

(A) Your opponent throws a right punch to your face. (B) Move your right palm across your chest, right to left, to deflect your opponent's fist to your left. (C&D) As your opponent counters with a left punch, drop into a horse stance and raise your right forearm to parry his punch up and out. Follow immediately with an open hand strike at your opponent's head, using the edge of your palm to strike with.

FORM

(72) With your feet remaining in place, rotate your right forearm (not shown) clockwise (so that your right palm passes in front of your face) until your palm is at your waist. (73) Thrust a right tiger claw strike outward at face level. (74) Retract your right hand into the ready position on the hip, closing your fist as you retract your hand.

APPLICATION

(A&B) As your opponent steps forward with a right punch to your head, swing your right forearm clockwise while pivoting your upper body to the right, deflecting his punch outside and to your right. (A&B should be one smooth motion.) (C) Continue circling your right forearm downward, forcing your opponent's arm away and leaving an opening. (D) Thrust a right tiger claw strike to your opponent's jaw, snapping his head back.

75

FORM

Note: Steps 78 and 79 are a mirror image of steps 56-58, with your stance on the opposite leg; the sequence remains identical.

(75) Step with your right leg across your left leg into a scissors stance. (76) Step with your left leg into a left forward stance. (77) Slide your right leg back, pivoting to the right on your left foot and assuming the ready position. (78) Step forward with your right foot facing 45 degrees to your left into a scissors stance. (79) Raise your left leg until the knee is at waist level (not shown) then thrust your left leg out with a kick at knee level.

77

APPLICATION

See the application for steps 56-58 on page 47.

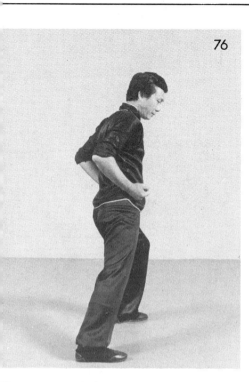

FORM

Note: Steps 80-89 are a mirror image of steps 59-68, with the hand motions performed with your opposite hand, and your stance on the opposite leg; the sequence remains identical.

(80) Cock your left leg again, then step out into a forward stance, still facing 45 degrees to your left. At the same time, thrust your right palm down in an arc. (81) Rotate your right forearm clockwise until your palm is directly in front of your body. (82) Retract your right palm toward your right shoulder. (83) Thrust your right palm straight out. Repeat steps 82 and 83 two more times. (84) Draw your right palm back until your palm is near your right ear. (85) Thrust your right forearm in a downward arc. (86) Thrust your right hand straight out, fully extending your right arm until your fingers are at eye level. (87) Snap your wrist downward, forming the tiger claw. (88) With your feet in place, shift back into a horse stance, simultaneously raising the left palm across your chest blocking outward, 45 degrees to your left. (89) Shift back into a left forward stance, simultaneously thrusting straight out with a right tiger claw.

APPLICATION

See the application for steps 59-68 on pages 50 and 51.

FORM

Note: Steps 90-98 are a mirror image of steps 69-77, with the hand motions performed with your opposite hand, and your stance on the opposite leg; the sequence remains identical.

(90) Shift into a horse stance, simultaneously moving your left palm across in a downward block and drawing the right fist back to your right side at the waist. (91) Lift your left forearm up and outward, then (92) swing your left forearm in a downward arc to your right, palm up at chest level. (93) Rotate your left forearm counterclockwise (so that your left palm passes in front of your face) until your palm is at your waist. (94) Thrust your left tiger claw outward at face level. (95) Retract your left hand into the ready position on your hip, closing your fist as you retract your hand. (96) Step with your left leg across your right leg into a scissors stance. (97) Step out with your left leg into a left forward stance facing 45 degrees to your right. (98) Slide your left leg back, pivoting on your right foot and assuming the ready position.

APPLICATION

See the application for steps 69-77 on pages 53 and 55.

91 92

94 95

97 98

FORM

(99) Shift your left foot to the left until your feet are shoulder-width apart, then (100-102) raise your right leg and execute a front kick at knee level.

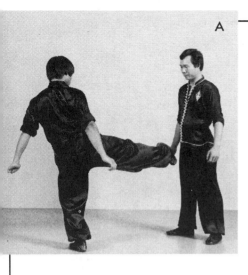

A

B

APPLICATION

(A) Your opponent throws a right front kick at your groin. (B-D) Evade his kick by sidestepping to your left and executing a front kick to his exposed knee.

C

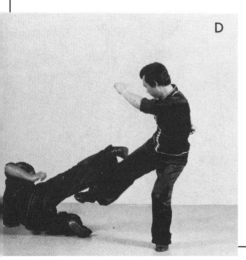

D

FORM

(103-105) Step forward with your right leg, bring your left knee up and propel yourself forward, jumping off your right leg and extending your right leg so that you land (106) in a forward stance, thrusting both hands downward at a 45-degree angle. (107) Thrust both your hands upward, bringing your palms together above your body and keeping your elbows bent. Your head should be between your extended arms. (108) Shift back into a horse stance, moving your left foot slightly to the left and drawing your right leg back. Simultaneously, pull both hands straight back toward each shoulder in the tiger claw position. (109) Shift into a forward stance, simultaneously thrusting both palms forward in a strike.

106

107

104

105

108

109

APPLICATION

(A&B) As your opponent throws a front kick toward your knees or groin, shift your left leg back into a forward stance and thrust both arms downward, deflecting his leg with your left forearm. (C-E) As your opponent counters with a double roundhouse strike toward your head, thrust both hands upward (maintaining your stance) in a finger strike to your opponent's eyes, simultaneously blocking his attack with the outside of your forearms. (F&G) Shift into a horse stance while grasping your opponent's arms, pulling him off balance and separating his arms to give you another opening. (H) Shift your weight forward into a right forward stance and thrust your palms in a strike to your opponent's collarbone (see inset).

FORM

(110) Pull your right leg back into a cat stance while pulling both hands back and downward in a diagonal motion across your body, such that the hands cross each other before ending up palms down by your hips. Note they are still in the tiger claw position. (111) Step with the right leg into a forward stance while thrusting both fists straight out. The striking surface is the row of knuckles nearest the thumb.

APPLICATION

(A&B) As your opponent attempts a finger strike to your throat, drop back on your left foot to avoid his attack, then bring both forearms up outside of his arms. (C) Shift into a cat stance, rolling your hands inside your opponent's arms and pushing them out and away. By shifting your weight you have also drawn him forward off balance. (D) Thrust both fists in a strike at your opponent's eyes.

69

FORM

(112) Slide your right foot to the right, then your left foot forward and to the left, so that you are in a horse stance, your chest facing the same direction as step 111. As your left foot moves into position, turn your head to the left and move your left palm from right to left, sliding it outside your right fist as you draw your right fist back to your hip. (113) Shift into a left forward stance facing 90 degrees to your left and execute a straight punch with your right fist. (114) Step forward with your right leg into a horse stance, at the same time lifting your right forearm in an upward block. Note that you are now facing 45 degrees to the left relative to your position in step 113. (115) Swing your right palm in a downward arc toward your chest and draw your left palm across your chest to your right forearm. (116) Shift your weight back into a forward stance, simultaneously executing a right forearm block above your head and thrusting your left palm straight out.

113

115

116

APPLICATION

Note: This application shows steps 110-116 when you are facing more than one opponent.

(A) You are confronted by three opponents. (B) As the opponent to your immediate right attempts to grab your throat, shift back into a cat stance, increasing the distance between you and him. At the same time, deflect his arms outward. (C&D) Draw both your hands back toward your hips, pulling your opponent off balance, then thrust both fists straight forward in a strike to your opponent's eyes. (E-G) As the opponent to your left throws a straight left punch, shift into a horse stance and deflect his punch with your left hand and follow with a straight right punch to his solar plexus. (H-J) The last opponent attacks with a left punch to your head. Block his punch outward with your right hand, then use the outside edge of your hand, palm up, to strike your opponent's throat.

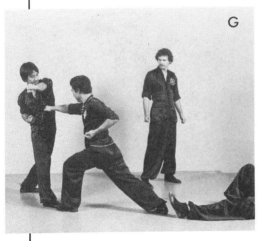

FORM

(117) Pull your right foot back into a cat stance, simultaneously pulling your left fist back in a short, counterclockwise motion into the position shown, and drop your right elbow in toward your body, bent at a 45-degree angle. (118) Step forward with your right foot into a forward stance and drop your fists in a downward strike.

APPLICATION

(A) As your opponent throws a straight right punch. (B) Pull back into a cat stance, drawing your left fist and forearm back to deflect your opponent's punch outward. (C) Using both fists simultaneously, strike downward into your opponent's face.

FORM

(119) Execute a right uppercut, dropping your left fist behind you. (120) Execute a left uppercut, dropping your right fist behind you. (121) Shift into a horse stance while pulling your left fist back to your hip and execute a straight punch with your right. (122) Shift back into a right forward stance and execute a straight left punch.

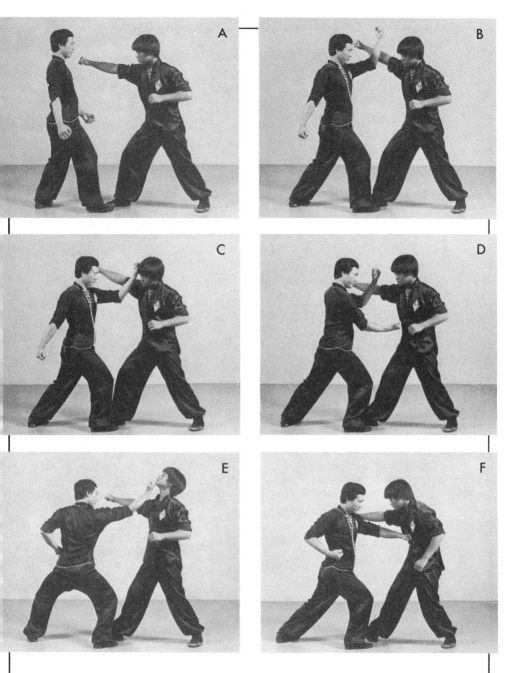

APPLICATION

(A&B) As your opponent throws a straight right punch, raise your left forearm upward to block your opponent's punch to the outside, then (C) use the same arm to deliver a left fist strike downward to his head. (D&E) Execute an uppercut strike with your right fist. (F) Follow through with a straight left punch.

FORM

(123) Pivot 180 degrees to your left on the balls of your feet into a horse stance, delivering a right-to-left block with your left palm. (124) Shift into a left forward stance and execute a straight right punch. (125) Step forward with your right leg into a horse stance and raise your right forearm up in a block. (126) Swing your right arm in a downward arc, palm up, while drawing your left hand, palm down, toward your right elbow. (127) Shift into a right forward stance and thrust your left palm forward, simultaneously blocking upward with your right fore-

Continued on next page

arm. (128) Draw your right foot back into a cat stance, at the same time pulling your left fist up in a short, counterclockwise motion and your right fist down toward your body. (129) Step forward into a right forward stance and drop both fists in a downward strike. (130) Execute a right uppercut punch. (131) Execute a left uppercut punch. (132) Shift into a horse stance while pulling your left fist back toward your hip and execute a right punch. (133) Shift back into a right forward stance and execute a left punch.

APPLICATION

See the applications for steps 112-122 on pages 72, 73, 75 and 77.

129

130

132

133

FORM

(134) Move your left foot toward your right foot into a cat stance position while striking downward at a 45-degree angle with your left hand, arm extended. (135) Maintain the same stance and raise your left hand up in an arc, palm in toward your left ear. (136) Lift your left knee toward your chest. (137) Jump up, rotating your torso 180 degrees counterclockwise and swinging your right fist downward (138) as you land in a crouched position. (139) Move your right foot into a forward stance, shifting your weight forward and thrusting your right fist upward (clenched, using the eye of the phoenix). Your left fist (also in the eye of the phoenix position) is thrust horizontally across your chest at the same time.

135

136

138

139

APPLICATION

(A&B) As your opponent attempts a low kick to your left knee, shift into a cat stance (drawing your left foot back away from his attack) and strike downward with your left hand to block his kick. (C) As he counters with a straight right punch, block upward with your left hand. (D) As your opponent cocks his left leg for another kick, lift your left leg in anticipation and (E) jump up, using your left hand to strike downward and block his front kick. Landing on your left foot, strike downward (F) with your right fist to deflect his right punch. (G) Step forward with your right foot and use your right forearm to control your opponent's arm. (H) Strike his solar plexus with your left fist and his head with your right fist simultaneously.

FORM

(140) Pull your right leg back and shift into a cat stance. Simultaneously, rotate your left arm counterclockwise, left hand in a tiger claw position, and move your right hand across your chest from right to left. (141) Step with your left leg into a forward stance and thrust both hands (in the tiger claw position) outward, left hand low, right hand high.

APPLICATION

(A) Your opponent steps forward with a straight left punch to the face. (B) Shift back into a cat stance while deflecting the punch by rotating your left hand counterclockwise down on top of his punch. At the same time, your right hand is brought across your chest to guard against an elbow strike. (C) Step forward, using your right forearm to push his left arm down and away, until you can (D) execute a right tiger claw to his face and a left tiger claw to his groin.

FORM

(142) Move your palms back toward your left side, dropping your right fore-arm until it is parallel with the ground. Begin pivoting 45 degrees to your right (143) as you move your right leg into a cat stance. (144) Continue pivoting to the right and step into a right forward stance while thrusting out with your left palm (tiger claw position) and downward with your right palm. (145) Draw your palms toward your right side (the opposite of step 142) and (146) move your left leg back into a cat stance, pivoting 45 degrees to your left and reaching out with your left palm. (147) Pull your left palm down and back toward your left hip while si-multaneously striking forward with a right tiger claw.

APPLICATION

(A&B) The opponent closest to you attacks with a right punch. Move your left leg back and use your left forearm to deflect his punch, dropping your right forearm on top of his forearm at the same time. (C&D) Use your right hand to push your opponent's elbow to your right and follow through with a tiger claw strike to his face. (E&F) As the second opponent attacks with a left straight punch, step back with your right foot into a horse stance and deflect his punch by blocking with your left forearm, left to right. (G-I) By circling your left forearm clockwise, you will deflect his arm to your left. Step forward with your left leg and execute a tiger claw strike to his face with your right hand.

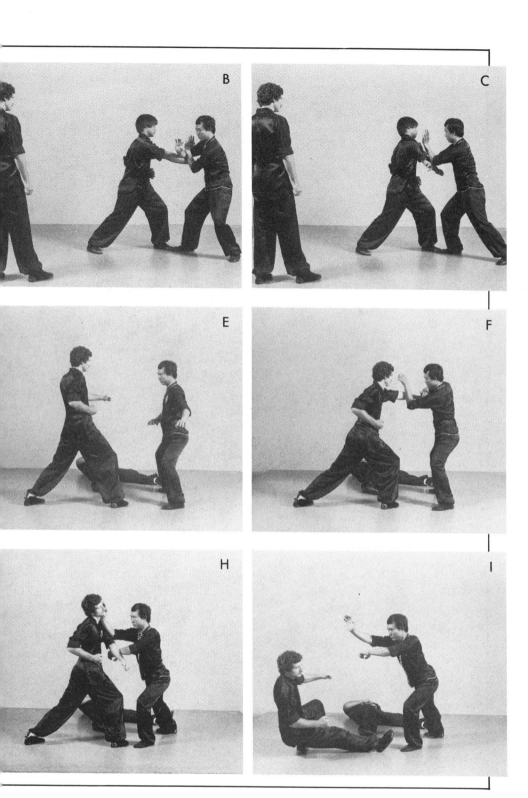

FORM

(148) Pull your left foot back to your right and your right hand back to your waist, facing 90 degrees to your right. (149) Move your right leg sideways into a horse stance, while your right hand executes a palm block parallel to the ground from right to left. (150) Pivot to your right into a front stance and push your right forearm out from your chest, executing a left tiger claw strike. (151) Step back with your left leg, pivoting into a scissors stance. (152) Step forward with your left foot into a cat stance while you pull the left tiger claw down and back toward your left hip in a grabbing motion and strike outward with a right tiger claw.

APPLICATION

(A) As your opponent throws a straight right punch, use your left forearm to deflect his punch down, while using your right hand to grab his elbow. (B) Pull his right elbow across your body toward his to bind him up, thrusting with a left tiger claw strike to his face. (C) Drop your left hand down

on the inside of his elbow. (D) As your other opponent attempts to close the distance for a punch, use your left hand to pull your opponent toward your left while you shift your weight onto your right leg. (E&F) Use a right tiger claw strike to throw your first opponent at your second opponent, knocking them both down.

FORM

(153) Pull your right hand straight back and (154) with your left leg step to your right into a scissors stance, lifting your right forearm in an upward arc. (155) Step with your right leg into a forward stance and push your right forearm straight out from your chest, simultaneously thrusting with a left tiger claw. (156) Pull your left leg forward next to your right foot, pivoting to your left and drawing your hands back to your hips. (157) Step back with your left leg into a horse stance while cutting downward at a 45-degree angle with your left forearm. Bring your forearm back into the position shown by bending it at the elbow. (158) Pivot into a left forward stance and thrust your right tiger claw straight out and your left forearm out (opposite of step 155).

APPLICATION

(A) As your opponent threatens with a left punch, (B) pivot to your right and use your left forearm to block his punch. (C) Slide your left hand up your opponent's arm just above the elbow. (D) Step forward with your left leg at a 45-degree angle into a horse stance, simultaneously using your left hand

to push your opponent's elbow toward his body. (E&F) Shift into a forward stance and deliver a right tiger claw strike to your opponent's face, knocking him away.

Note: Insets 1&2 show the proper grab and push motion used in this technique.

FORM

(159) Pull your right foot next to your left foot, pivoting to your right and drawing both hands back to your hips. (160) Step forward with your left leg and rotate your left forearm counterclockwise. (161) Draw your left hand in the tiger claw position straight back and thrust forward with a right tiger claw. (162) Step with your right foot into a cat stance while drawing your right tiger claw straight back in a grabbing motion and thrusting your left tiger claw forward.

APPLICATION

(A) As your opponent attempts a straight right punch, drop your right foot back and block with your left hand in a counterclockwise motion, deflecting it to the outside. (B) When your opponent shifts into a horse stance to deliver a left punch, draw your right hand up as you shift into a cat stance (C) blocking downward in a counterclockwise arc to deflect his punch. Your opponent's fist is now trapped beneath your elbow (see insets 1&2). (D) Follow immediately with a tiger claw thrust to your opponent's chin.

101

FORM

(163) Retract your left hand to your hip. (164) Step across your left leg with your right into a scissors stance, drawing your left palm across your chest. (165) Step out with your left leg into a forward stance, pushing your left forearm out and thrusting a right tiger claw forward. (166) Draw your right foot to your left, pivoting to your right and pulling both hands back to your hips. (167) Step across your right leg with your left into a scissors stance, pushing your right palm across your chest from right to left. (168) Step out with your right foot into a forward stance, pushing your right forearm straight out and thrusting with a left tiger claw. (169) Draw your left leg up to your right and retract your hands to your hips. (170) Step out with your right leg into a scissors stance, pushing your left palm from left to right across your chest. (171) Step out with your left leg into a forward stance, pushing your left forearm out and your right tiger claw straight out.

APPLICATION

The applications of these blocks, strikes and stances are shown in the application sections throughout the book.

FORM

(172) Step backward with your left leg into a forward stance, at the same time swinging both arms (fully extended, palms facing out) horizontally to your right; as they pass in front of your body retract them toward your chest and close your fists. (173) Repeat step 172 on the opposite side, stepping backward with your right leg into a forward stance and moving your arms in the same manner. (174) Step with your right leg across your left into a scissors stance while drawing your fists back to your hips. (175) Step with your left leg across your right into a scissors stance. (176) Step with your right leg into a forward stance, moving your left arm across your chest from right to left. (177) Pull your left hand straight back toward your chest, your right fist tucked against your chest. (178) Thrust out with your left forearm in an arc parallel to the ground (your hand in the tiger claw position), and swing your right fist straight back. (179) Pivot 180 degrees to your left (your feet remain stationary), swinging your left fist downward and your right fist upward. (180) Pivot back to the right, circling your right forearm and fist back to your hip while punching straight out with the left fist.

173

174

176

177

179

180

APPLICATION

(A&B) As your opponent threatens with a left punch, shift into a right forward stance at a right angle to your opponent and block his punch to the outside with a left tiger claw. (C&D) As your opponent throws a right punch, lift your left forearm to deflect that punch to the outside. (E) Pivoting into a left forward stance, swing your right arm in an upward arc, striking his arm beneath the elbow while your left arm continues to push his arm down. (F&G) As your opponent retracts his right arm and attempts another left punch, draw your right forearm up to block his punch to the outside. (H&I) Pivot to the right again as you deliver a left punch to his head.

B

C

E

F

H

I

181

FORM

Note: Steps 182-188 are a mirror image of steps 174-180 with the hand motions performed with your opposite hand and your stance on your opposite leg; the sequence remains identical.

(181) Swing your left forearm in toward your chest parallel to the ground. (182) Step with your left leg across your right into a scissors stance, drawing your left fist back to your hip. (183) Step with your right leg across your left into a scissors stance. (184) Step with your left leg into a forward stance, sweeping your right arm out from right to left and pushing your left palm across your chest from left to right. (185) Pull your right arm back toward your chest, your left fist tucked against your chest. (186) Thrust your right arm out in a tiger claw and swing your left fist straight back. (187) Pivot 180 degrees to your right (your feet remain stationary), swinging your right fist down and back and your left fist upward. (188) Pivot back to your left, circling your left forearm and fist back to your hip while punching straight out with your right fist.

183

186

APPLICATION

See the application for steps 174-180 on pages 106 and 107.

FORM

(189) Circle your right forearm toward your body, with your right hand in the crane's beak position. (190) Pivot to your right into a cat stance, simultaneously striking outward with your left hand in the crane's beak position. (191) Draw your left forearm directly back (bending at the elbow) and (192-194) pivot to your left into cat stance, simultaneously drawing the right hand back to strike and your left forearm in toward your chest. Strike outward with your right hand and then draw it back. (195) Begin shifting your weight to your left foot and cross your forearms in front of your chest as you (196) raise your right leg and spread your hands down and out to your sides, (197) executing a front kick. (Your position is the same as in step 196; the camera angle has shifted to show the kick.)

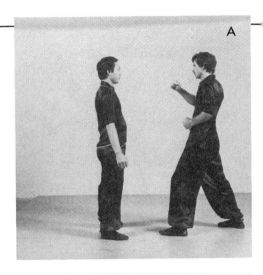

APPLICATION

(A&B) As your opponent throws a right punch, pivot to your right (without shifting your feet) and deflect his punch down by bringing your right forearm down onto his wrist. (C) Pivot to your left into a cat stance while using your crane's beak to hook your opponent's forearm and push it away from you. (D) Strike to his eyes with a left crane's beak. (E&F) Retract your left forearm to guard against his right elbow, then pivot to your right into a crane stance as he tries a left counter-punch. Block his forearm in the same manner using your left crane's beak to hook and parry. (G) Use your right crane's beak to strike your opponent's temple. (H&I) Retract your right forearm and drop it down and out, deflecting his arm and leaving him open for (J) a front kick to the groin.

FORM

(198) Retract your right leg while swinging your left crane's beak downward in an arc. (199) Step forward with your right foot into a forward stance and strike downward with your right crane's beak. (200) Withdraw your right crane's beak and (201) shift your weight onto your right foot in preparation for a (202) left front kick. (203) Retract your left leg as you strike downward with your right crane's beak, then (204) step down with your left foot into a forward stance and strike downward with a left crane's beak. (205) Shift your weight into a horse stance. (Note: The position of your feet has not changed from step 204, only the camera angle has changed). Swing your left forearm in a downward clockwise motion parallel to the ground. (206) Pivot to the left into a forward stance and block upward with the left forearm while executing a straight punch with your right. Use the eye of the phoenix fist.

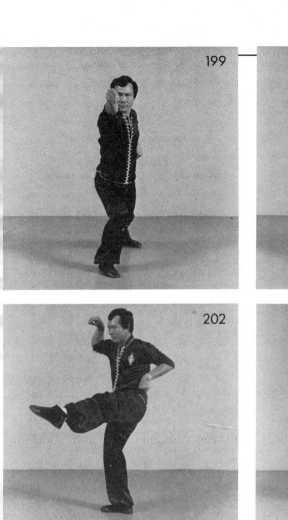

APPLICATION

(A) As your opponent throws a straight left punch, use a right forearm block (from left to right) to deflect his punch. (B&C) With your right leg, execute a front kick to your opponent's groin, which he blocks by dropping into a horse stance and using a

sweeping forearm block. (D) Swing your left arm down, using a crane's beak to parry your opponent's right arm out and execute (E) a right crane's beak strike to his eyes. Your opponent parries with a left forearm block. (F) Step forward with a left front kick,

Continued on next page

which he deflects (G) by stepping back into a scissors stance and blocking with a right forearm block. (H) Use a right crane's beak to push your opponent's arm to the right, then step forward with your left foot with a left crane strike to his eyes, which he parries

(I) with a right forearm block. (J) Pivot to your right into a horse stance to avoid his left punch to your midsection. (K) Deflect his right arm outside with a left forearm block and (L) step forward with a left straight punch to his exposed ribs.

FORM

(207) Shifting back into a horse stance, swing your right forearm across your body in a downward arc, drawing your left fist back to your hip. (208) Shift into a right forward stance and execute an upward block with the right forearm and a left punch (both hands are in the eye of the phoenix). (209) Step straight back with your right leg across your left into a scissors stance, swinging your right fist downward and keeping your left arm parallel to your chest. (210) Pivot 180 degrees into a horse stance, then (211) shift your weight into a left forward stance, executing two punches simultaneously, your right fist near the top of your head and your left fist at knee height.

APPLICATION

(A&B) As you lean toward your left to avoid a straight punch, draw your right forearm back and swing it clockwise to deflect your opponent's punch to the outside, then follow with (C) a punch to his solar plexus. (D) As he tries to counter with a side kick to your exposed right knee, (E) evade his kick by stepping back with your right leg into a scissors stance, simultaneously striking downward with your right fist to deflect his kick. (F&G) Immediately spin to your left by pivoting on both feet and execute a double strike to his throat and groin.

FORM

(212) Step slightly forward and to the right (your right leg pointed 90 degrees to the right relative to step 211), keeping both fists in position, then (213) pivot into a left forward stance while executing an outward left block and a straight right punch. (214) Draw your right heel next to your left, spreading your arms, then (215) step with your left foot across your right foot into a scissors stance, simultaneously swinging both forearms down until they cross in front of your midsection, left wrist over right. (216) Move your right heel next to your left heel (remaining at the same height as step 215), drop your left foot straight back and pivot your upper body into a left forward stance. Your fists remain crossed at the wrist. (217) Shift back to your right into a forward stance, swinging both arms at full extension, your right arm in an upward arc, your left arm downward in the opposite direction.

213

214

216

217

APPLICATION

(A&B) As your opponent throws a right roundhouse kick, (C) block with your left forearm, pivoting to the left to get under his kick and (D) counter with a right punch to his exposed groin. (E&F) If your opponent fakes with the kick and instead throws a left punch to the face, counter with a right forearm block (supported by your left arm), deflecting from right to left and then stepping forward with your right leg (G) and swing your right forearm outward, striking his neck.

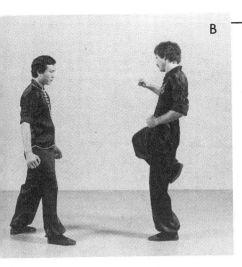

B

D

E

G

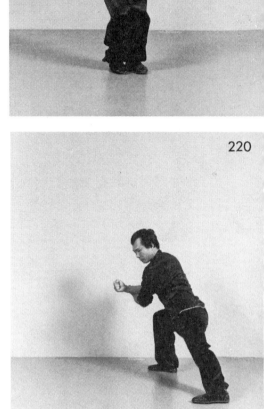

218

FORM

(218) Bring your left heel forward next to your right, then (219) step with your right foot across your left into a scissors stance, crossing your forearms (right wrist over left) in front of you. (220) Move your left heel next to your right (remaining at the same height as step 219), then step straight back with your right foot, pivoting to the right into a forward stance. Your arms remain crossed. (221) Shift back into a left forward stance, sweeping your arms at full extension, your left fist in an upward arc, your right down and behind you. (222) Step slightly forward and to the right into a right forward stance,

220

Continued on next page

223

crossing your forearms. (223) With your left hand in the tiger claw position, strike outward in a horizontal arc (swinging your right arm back simultaneously). (224) Take one step forward with both feet. Pivot to your left by stepping out with your left foot at a 45-degree angle to your last position. Swing your arms at full extension (like a windmill), left fist downward, right fist upward. Both fists should pass directly in front of your face. (225) Step forward 45 degrees to your right into a forward stance and repeat the two-arm swing, this time with your left fist swinging upward, your right fist down and back. (226) Step forward 45 degrees to your left into a left forward stance, swinging your left fist in a downward arc behind you and your right fist in a downward arc in front of you. (227) Step 45 degrees to your right into a right forward stance, swinging your right fist back up along the same arc as step 226 until it is behind your head, and swing your left fist in an uppercut motion along the same path. (228) Pivot to your left into a forward stance and execute a right punch as you retract your left hand to your waist.

226

APPLICATION

(A&B) As your opponent throws a right punch, block in a counterclockwise motion with your left forearm, deflecting his punch downward (C) as you bring your right forearm up to scissor (D) your opponent's elbow. (E&F) As he retracts his right fist and tries to counter with a left punch, block his punch with your right arm (G&H) as you shift your weight into a right forward stance to add power to your left uppercut to his chin. (I&J) Now shift to your left and execute a straight right punch to your opponent's midsection.

FORM

(229) Maintaining your forward stance, push both palms straight out from your chest. (230) Slide your right foot forward while drawing your right palm back toward your hip and your left palm from left to right across your chest. (231) Slide your right foot back to its position in step 229 and again thrust your palms out from your chest. (232) Shift your weight to your right into a forward stance and swivel your right forearm clockwise in front of your chest, bringing your fist back to your hip as you execute a straight left punch. (233) Maintaining your position, push both palms straight out from your chest. (234) Slide your left foot forward while drawing your left palm back toward your hip and your right palm from right to left across your chest. (235) Slide your left foot back to its position in step 233 and thrust both palms out again.

APPLICATION

(A&B) As your opponent throws a right punch, step forward and deflect his punch outward with your left forearm. (C) Execute a straight palm strike with your right hand to your opponent's head, who shifts to evade the strike. (D) Use your right palm to grasp the opponent's neck from behind and to pull him toward you. Slide your right foot forward simultaneously to attempt a sweep. (E&F) Your opponent lifts his leg to avoid the sweep and steps forward attempting to free himself. (G) Disengage your right palm and pull it back toward your waist, then (H&I) slide your right foot between his legs as you thrust your palm forward against his chest, throwing him backward.

FORM

(236) Pivot to your right into a forward stance, simultaneously swinging your right elbow in an upward arc and moving your left forearm outward parallel to the ground. (237) Step with your right leg into a forward stance at a 90-degree angle and thrust both palms out, left over right.

APPLICATION

(A) As your opponent steps in with a right punch, shift your stance and use your right elbow to deflect his punch, immediately dropping your right forearm (B) down onto his arm with your palm just above his right elbow. (C) As you use your right palm to push his right arm in toward his body, step forward with your right leg and (D) follow through with a tiger claw strike to his face.

238

FORM

(238) Step back across your left leg with your right leg into a scissors stance, simultaneously swinging your right tiger claw outward and pulling your left forearm across your chest. (239&240) Pull both arms in to your chest and pivot to your left into a horse stance. (241) Strike outward with both fists in a downward arc. (242) Slide your right foot in a right-to-left arc into a forward stance while using the right fist for a roundhouse strike.

240

APPLICATION

(A) As your opponent throws a right punch, retreat by stepping back with your right leg into a scissors stance and pivot to your left (B&C) as he attempts to follow through with a left punch. (D) Deflect his punch by striking

out and down with your left fist, then step forward (E) with your right leg and execute a roundhouse punch to the back of his head (your knuckles are the point of contact). Note that your left arm is still checking his left.

FORM

(243) Thrust your left hand out in a tiger claw strike. (244) Shift your weight into a horse stance and execute a straight right punch. (245) Step back across your left leg with your right leg into a scissors stance, crossing your forearms in front of your body (left over right). (246&247) Step forward with your left foot, then jump into the air, spinning 180 degrees to your right and swinging both arms outward in a large, arcing motion. (248) Land in a scissors stance, arms behind you.

244

245

247

248

APPLICATION

(A&B) As your opponent springs forward with a right side kick, (C) jump back and spread your arms to avoid his kick and land

(D) in a scissors stance, swinging your right arm outward to deflect his kick. (Your hands are tucked in the crane's beak position.)

249

250

FORM

(249) Rotate your upper body into a scissors stance, moving your right forearm outward in an arc. (250) Shift your weight into a horse stance while executing a left uppercut and lifting the right palm overhead to block. (251) Shift your weight again into a left scissors stance and deliver a right uppercut while raising your left palm overhead to block.

251

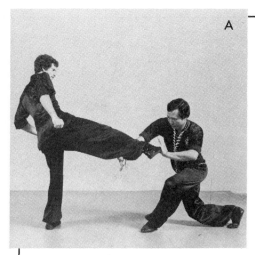

APPLICATION

(A) As your opponent throws a front kick, drop back into a scissors stance and swing your right forearm from right to left to deflect his kick to your left. (Use your left palm to prevent his right foot from penetrating too far if your block is late.) (B&C) Shift back into a horse stance as your opponent attempts a left roundhouse strike and block his punch upward with your right forearm and palm, bringing your left fist up simultaneously to (D) deliver a left uppercut to his chin.

FORM

(252) Step forward at a 45-degree angle to your left into a right scissors stance, simultaneously sweeping both palms down to your right. (253) Step forward with your left leg into a scissors stance, rotating your left palm counterclockwise in toward your hip and sweeping your right palm from right to left across your chest. (254) Step with your right leg into a forward stance and thrust both palms forward, right over left. Now, repeating the motions on the opposite side, (255) step forward with your left leg into a scissors stance and sweep both palms down toward your left. (256) Step forward with your right leg into a scissors stance, pulling your right palm in toward your hip and sweeping your left palm from left to right across your chest. (257) Step with your left leg into a forward stance and thrust both palms forward, left over right.

253

254

256

257

A

B

APPLICATION

(A) As your opponent attempts a right front kick, step to your left away from the attack into a scissors stance and slash downward with your right forearm to deflect his kick. (B&C) As your second opponent steps in with a right

punch, circle your right hand up clockwise to deflect his punch and bring your left forearm across your body to check his elbow. (D) Step forward with your left leg and strike simultaneously at his throat and groin.

FORM

(258) Draw your right foot back and twist your body into a scissors stance. At the same time, thrust your right tiger claw outward and bring your left fist straight back and above your head. (259) Rise up on your left leg and simultaneously execute a right front kick and a downward knuckle strike with your left hand. (*Note:* The camera angle has been changed; your body is still facing in the same direction as step 258). Retract the right leg, then (260) step forward into a right forward stance. Thrust both palms straight out in a double tiger claw strike. (261) Draw your right foot back into a cat stance while pulling both palms down and back toward your hips in a grabbing motion. (262) Step forward again into a right forward stance and thrust both fists forward.

APPLICATION

(A) As your opponent steps forward with a right punch, swing your right forearm up clockwise to deflect his punch, simultaneously raising your left fist. (B) Use your right palm to grab his right arm at the wrist and pull him toward you off balance, simultaneously raising your right leg for a (C) front kick to his groin.

At the same time, strike downward with your left fist, using your knuckles to strike his eyes. (D) For a finishing blow, step forward with your right leg and deliver a double tiger claw strike to his collarbone. Use a snapping motion of the wrists for a strong downward pull.

D

FORM

(263) Step back with your right leg into a horse stance. Draw your right fist back to your waist, palm up, and keep your left palm thrust outward in a tiger claw position. (264) Shift your weight into a left forward stance and execute a straight right punch. (265) Move your right foot to your right and pivot to your right while retracting your right fist and sweeping your left palm across your chest from left to right. (266) Move your left leg back into a cat stance, drawing your left hand back from right to left (palm out) and executing a right punch. (267) Bring your heels together and draw your fists in toward your chest, elbows out. (268) Circle both fists in a downward arc to your waist, palms up. (Steps 266-268 are identical to steps 4-6 of the opening salute.)

266

APPLICATION

The applications of these blocks, strikes and stances are shown in the application sections throughout the book.

264

265

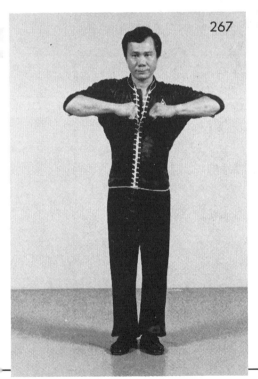

267

268